Through Me to Me

Through Me to Me

Kay T. Smith

To order additional copies of this book, contact:
Xlibris
1-888-795-4274
www.Xlibris.com
Orders@Xlibris.com
787166

Acknowledgement

To my son; you are my heart and a true gift from God. You have ministered to me from such a young age and I am grateful to God for you. To Pat; thank you for believing in me and for helping me to "cross the street." To everyone that has read or allowed me to read my pieces to them and encouraged me to share this gift; thank you for being vessels of God. You are greatly appreciated....

God is faithful; I trust Him!

Kay

Contents

Struggle…

Love...

Influences...

Growth...

Struggle…

No One Bothers

Kay Smith

Invisible tears became visible today
Silent suffering became static
The fight inside became fear
and gave way to any chance of freedom,
But no one bothers to really see…
Eagles soar, dolphins dive
into their places of freedom
To fly and swim another day
They are connected to each other
We are dysfunctional so
No one bothers to really see…

Through Me.....To Me

Finding me has been exhausting to say the least
It's been an emotional trip to hell and back
and I have been the feast
To deposit something positive into just one life
Has only been the goal of one
and that's the living Christ
Through HIM and only HIM alone
Cause there has been no other
Is the reason that I've grown
Not brother, sister, father
and no not even mother
I think of those that have support of
praying friends and family
I'd get so angry deep inside
wondering who was there for me
We cannot choose our parents,
We cannot choose our sibs
But we can choose our course in life
and we can forgive
All of those who had a chance,
But just would not invest
Into the life of an innocent child
That went from lost to blessed
Its taken over forty years,
I've walked this path alone
On a biological quest to reconnect
with those that were my own
But what I've come to realize
in searching for my folks
is that sometimes you must let go

of those that are unequally yoked
I can't go back and change the past
For it has been my test
But Christ has been there all the time
and I am more not less
With or without my family I have finally grown
From this exhausting trip to find me
and I didn't have to do it alone
The hand of Christ was on my life from very early on
HIS amazing mercy and HIS grace has kept me all along
And so I will continue the journey to find me
And learn to invest into myself and be completely free

Who Will Fight For Me?

Kay Smith

My life, my issues, so unwanted......
Who will fight for me?
On my own from birth til now
Who fought for me?
To make it this far, I don't know how
So much pain in just one life
For a daughter, sister, mother, aunt and wife
Who has fought for me?
Soiled from birth by a curious boy
Private parts used as a toy
All in fun, but a
downward spiral has begun
Who fought for me?
So sincere, so eager to please
Revolving door relationships just a tease
My mother's love? Obligation.
My father's love? Consummation.
My sister's love? Brief flirtation.
My brother's love? Initiation....
Into a life of opened doors
Flood gates of hell, sexual scores
Who has fought for me?
You give your all, you give your heart
With carelessness it's torn apart
You hate yourself for giving in
No one stays, alone again
Who will fight for me?
You put up front, you play the game
But no one's there, just constant pain

No one knows, it's all the same
Will someone want me
Will someone stay
Will someone fight for me…I pray
I am the one who fights for everyone
Only to be dumped and dumped and dumped
each time
I give my heart to only find
there's no one there - ever
to fight ….. for me - never
Who will fight for me?

Questions

Kay Smith

Do you know what it's like to feel so empty
and alone, to give and not receive,
to love so much and never be loved, to want
to receive love from anywhere
Do you know what it's like to be so scared and so afraid
that it makes you not know who you are
To always feel rejected; to want to run
Do you know what it's like to try your
hardest and people still walk away
To completely give your all and it's never enough
To give someone your heart
only to receive it back
in a million shattered pieces
Do you know what it's like to always have to fight for yourself
And be so tired of it
To want someone on your side
Do you know what it's like to feel so ashamed and guilty
That you isolate yourself from life
Do you know what it's like?
I do.......
How do I proceed from here?

Who Knew?

Kay Smith

I never knew I was the enemy
I didn't have a clue
I never knew I wouldn't be loved
What's a soul to do
I never knew I would be dismissed
By each and everyone
Even my job let me go
Nine plus years and done
It came so fast
Without a blink or sound
I guess I am just so unique
No one wants me around
I never knew just how much
No one really cared
I understand, I finally do
Everything's been aired
Now I have a clue
What's a soul to do
Who knew?

Painful Memory

Kay Smith

I saw him today, he came into the store
I remembered, then cringed and experienced it
like it was 33 years before...only today is June 5, 2004
He wouldn't or couldn't look at me, I stared in disbelief
the innocence he stole from me just like a common thief
I wonder if he does recall those days of causing pain
of violation, humiliation, guilt and utter shame...
This little girl of 43 remembers every move done
as a grown man commenced to get his groove on
I watched his back today as he strolled out of the store
I remembered, then cringed and experienced it
like it was 33 years before.....only today is June 5, 2004

Life's Therapy

Kay Smith

Define.
Fix.

I know why
I am the way
I am

Define.
Fix.
Release.

How do I
go about this?

Define.
Fix.
Release.
Forgive.
?

Awakened

Kay Smith

Awakened, but not healed
The realization is fulfilled
I am the only me
She was the only her
My mother's emotional state
Just cannot dictate, see
I am the only me
and she was the only her
those past pangs of neglect
continue to reoccur
Awakened, but not healed
Yes, the realization is fulfilled
She is gone, I am alive
My healing has got to come
from inside of me
this is the reality
that the dictation
will come from my
emancipation sealed
awakened and finally healed.

Forgiveness

Kay Smith

She won't let go
or is it me
the forgiveness
has not come to settle
in my heart
I continue to struggle
with her inability to parent me
emotionally, this is an art

My Dance

Kay Smith

The beats of life are so diverse
but for these beats one cannot rehearse
the steady and consistent heartbeat of life
pulsating, beckoning, cold as ice
interrupted, pause, put on hold
staccato, vibrato, the snare drum roll
the trills, thrills, and all those runs
the bass, the pace, the beats undone
upbeats, downbeats, beats in between
depressed beats, up lifting beats, beats unseen
they can be felt when the vision is not clear
though not seen or heard still I can hear
the call of the diverse beats of my life
through turmoil, stress, trials and strife
captivating, exhilarating, intimidating and free
to enjoy each beat to the fullest, to be and explore
the beats of my life as consistent, vibrant and diverse as before
I will attempt to rehearse no more
Just sway and dance and yes enjoy....

Sigh

Kay Smith

Can't fly?
Spread your wings anyway
Wait and be prepared
Your gust of wind will come
You will fear, but
You will soar eventually
That eagle is in your soul

Peoples

Kay Smith

We just peoples is all
Bound by DNA
Not one emotional tie
I didn't choose them
and they didn't choose me
God – why you give me these peoples?
To make me strong?
To educate me?
To punish me?
I won't be bound by DNA
'**D**em **N**o good **A**ncestors!!!
We just peoples is all…

Downsized

Kay Smith

Life's transition is humbling
Evicted from a comfortable place
Pursuit of a new knowledge
Update the outdated
The man-child starts to bloom
The journey of a lifetime faced
Transition into freedom…

Perversion

Kay Smith

Perverted by choice?
No!!! No one heard my voice
telling, screaming, pleading
no…I don't like that or
perhaps no I don't know
if I want to get down like that
Did I misbehave?
Seemingly….
Made to feel like a slave
Abuse from the past cannot be laid
to rest, I've tried my best,
but to be perverted by force with no recourse
Is this a test to see if I will survive still me?
Who is that? Who am I?
I'd rather live than die so alone
Knowing that the choice was not my own
To be perverted, never pure love,
Never alerted to the sick and twisted freaks
Who take my sleep, I cannot weep for them or me
of course, the force is silent now
long forgotten by women and men yet in the end
I am only loved by a perverted race
of empty shells who
made my life a living hell
Can you hear me now?! Good!
I'm fighting back with all of me I can find

Of a woman-child left behind
with your choice to ignore my voice to force
innocence to become perverse to see the terseness
of it all come full circle
and I am still standing tall, unslaved and free
Perverted by choice?
No, not me

Weariness

Kay Smith

I am so tired of being strong; my soul just wants to rest
I live my life aching to belong, a never-ending quest
I'm never able to fit in, among, but not included
my place of comfort this has not been to this I have alluded
The pain of being so grown-up for the first part of my life
has left my inner most self weary from the strife
Just what do you do when all the energy is gone
The mere existence of a thought from the
past just makes it all prolonged
I look in the mirror so many days; I stare and fail to see
the little girl that never was and now can't ever be
In her place a woman stands, beat down from all the life
that was taken from her everyday with intensity and rife
It is said that you cannot miss what you never had
but never having a childhood this is very sad
I've lived my life from birth till now aching to belong
The never-ending quest must end; my spirit sings a new song
My soul just wants to rest; I am so tired of being strong

The Chase

Kay Smith

I saw you, so I reached out
I wanted a friend, you wanted more
The pursuit was intense
I resisted with fierceness
Reality sets in for me
My perfect world does not exist
In my mind I tried to go where you wanted
So I wouldn't lose you
I wanted the transference to be smooth
From my mind to your touch, only…
I didn't really want to be there
All I could see was the pattern repeating
Pursuit / Resistance
Retreat / Contemplate
Fear / Pain
Surrender / Regret
Abandoned / Alone
I saw another, so I built walls
I still wanted a friend, but reality set in
My perfect world does not exist

Stagnant

Kay Smith

I am a woman of 14
stuck, trapped and afraid
to progress any further
life continues on as if
you were meant to be here - 14 at 43
consistently afraid to experience
any feelings of love, acceptance, belonging
absorbed in the safety of walls
constructed with such determination to let no one enter in
only....no one leaves either
the 14-year-old continues on with life
as if she has been at this place forever
she sees and feels with the emotions of 14
yet she has the responsibilities of 43
complete with sexual expectations
and fringe benefits
only....she feels nothing
shhh.....lay still and receive the pain
as if it were first prize
you stare into the dark, then
close your eyes and let the silent tears flow
at 14 there is no experience of climax
just relief that one more time is done
I open my eyes and remember, I am 43
I have a child to raise, a home to attend to
I have been at this place forever
A woman of 14

Going it Alone

Kay Smith

Angry days are so painful
I have to disappear,
withdraw into my own existence,
the place I have made for me
NO!!! You cannot come…
You may get hurt there
for I cannot be responsible for you
in that place
You need to wait for me here
And pray that
I will return
renewed and healed
from the pain that caused the
angry days

The Emotions of D

Kay Smith

Depressed, disturbed, and distressed
Disgruntled and in despair
I pray and pray for relief
It seems as if no one cares

Demoralized and debased
Downtrodden and destitute
HIS mercy, grace and forgiving love
I must not refute

Disheartened, daft and duped
Defenseless, defected and dazed
That HE would go to Calvary
For me, I'm so amazed

Derelict, defunct and dense
Dwarfed, dogmatic and doomed
HIS perseverance for my soul
Began before the womb

And so I must delight
and dwell within HIS love
For when it seems that no one cares
My Father is above

The fight for me is detailed
planned by one divine
and yes my steps are ordered
It is not my will but thine

I will not be dismayed
It's not even up for debate
I will defy the one who devours
Your blood has cleaned the slate

And so my life is yours
this has been designed
Devoted and dedicated
Defeat? I must decline.

To Be....

Kay Smith

I never wanted to be this way
I exist, yet I don't
I feel so very deeply, yet I am numb
I desire more, but I accept what is
I rumble and roar, yet I crouch in fear
I am victorious, yet I am defeated
I hope no one hurts me, yet I wish a Negro would...
I fear rejection, yet I crave acceptance
I define for others, yet I confuse myself
I cringe at touch, yet I long for intimacy
I am quiet, yet I have so very much to say
Why am I this way? Sigh....
I never wanted to be this way

Cleansing

Kay Smith

As the shower washes over my tears
I try to recover from my thoughts
I try to regain consciousness
I try to process my sessions
I try to come down from the day
I watch as the drain swallows
all the cares of the day
If only I could leave them there
Eventually I would be completely clean.

Remember...

Kay Smith

I heard no words of comfort
I remember no words of wisdom
All I heard was silence
All I felt was loneliness
No "dry your eyes child,
put your tough skin back on"
You had 26 years to speak
You chose silence and seclusion
You chose to hold on to your shame and guilt
You took it to your grave
I choose to bury mine while I am alive
I'll leave memories of love, meaningful conversation
And words of wisdom for my child
My shame, guilt and fear won't silence me,
it won't own me.
I can't hear or remember from you
So I have to speak and make my own moments
I won't wait 26 years,
I won't make your choices
I won't mourn life
My child will hear and remember
Me.

If You Knew

Kay Smith

I wonder if you knew
What would you have done
I don't know that you would have responded at all
I think you knew, but it was the secret of "us"
The secret that was formed many years before
The secret that touched so many lives
in a way never to be forgotten
but not wanting to be remembered
Am I a survivor because you knew, but didn't act
If you knew would I have been worse off
Ostracized? Criticized? Penalized? Scandalized?
I wonder if it was because of my conception
Being conceived in shame and guilt breeds shame and guilt
I never knew you…but, we are bound by the secret of" us"
I wonder…if you knew.….

Perspective

Kay Smith

Pastor says:
When you have the wrong perspective
you replace contentment with resentment

Father's perspective –
Gone fishing with my son…a wasted day
Son's perspective –
Went fishing with my dad…best day of my life

I see my mother as a provider, as a man should be
She valued money and material things
instead of people, instead of her children

There was a man in the home physically,
but he was invisible in all other aspects
He took what should have been
my mother's most valued possessions –
her daughters

<u>She</u> provided as <u>he</u> should have and
<u>we</u> provided as <u>she</u> should have
dysfunction within dysfunction
became inevitable
my innocence became open season
for an eternity

Mother's perspective –
Working to provide for my children…best thing I could give them
My perspective –
Best thing my mom could've given me was
her physical touch and attention

Her contentment with her things
became a loss of both her daughters' spirit

My brief contentment with her things
became a lifetime of resentment for her things

Perspective…to be continued

The Friendship Meal

Kay Smith

People are pretenders, it happens everyday
If you're not what's in this week, they just throw you away
They see the decorative package all dressed from head to toe
the brim, the clothes, the purse and shoes and yes the lovely bow
They see you from the outside and proceed to check you out
to see just what the real deal is and what you're all about
and if they like what they see and think that you're worth knowing
then in your face they make their case; their personality glowing
They dangle the choicest bait to try to reel you in
you try to resist, but you just can't and so let the games begin
What you thought was going to be a simple little meal
became an enormous and complex carbohydrate deluxe ordeal
It became so hard to digest, it made you comatose
and once you came back to yourself you knew that you came close
to being devoured completely by this unsuspecting beast
that your kindness and good heart was about to be the feast
Getting to know people... it really is quite hard
you've constantly got to be on watch and learn to keep your guard
You go in so sincere, but then you realize
in trying to make a friend, that you've been super-sized
So if you have been sacrificed and taken advantage of too
learn to let go and forgive, there's a ram in the bush for you

burrrrp......ooh excuse me
I just had a friendship meal
Lord, please forgive me.......

The Walk

Kay Smith

I walk and pour my inner most thoughts out to you
In frustration I tell you my fears, my dreams,
and the desires of my heart
I see you as I look at the moon…it's as if you're following me
I see you when I look at the stars…too many too even number
I feel you brushing against me in the cool
midnight breeze; clearing my mind
I babble on like a brook; petitioning and beseeching you
for freedom from the bondage of my thoughts
The color has gone from the sky; faintly I see the clouds
the backdrop is now night; which represents sleep
You never sleep; the heavens are lit with your radiance
You are the light that slices through our darkest state of being
I walk to work out my issues; I walk for deliverance and freedom
Nature looks on as if to say – don't be afraid – just let go
Heaven will sustain you; God is your sustenance
It just doesn't work and I'm exhausted;
the famine has left me barren
The break through sits like the moon on the lake
its right there, but I cannot obtain it; it angers me
I cry in fear from uncertainty; I can't see the plan
I wrestle and struggle to be of sound mind
I give! I don't know what to do so…
I walk and pour my inner most thoughts out to you

The Gift of Life and Choice

Kay Smith

My life has truly been a gift.
You chose me before I was created in sin.
What satan meant to break my mother down,
you took and made the way for a new generation.

I tried to be so careful with the gift of new life that was given.
Many mistakes were made, yet you carried me to safety
so the gift would not become scarred in the processes
of my failures and journey to maturity.

For a small girl who never knew the feeling
of being loved or love itself;
the gift was the perfect answer for such an empty life.
As the gift of life matures, it gains new appreciation
for the small girl and the empty life she endured.

Amidst all the bumbling and stumbling and outright defiance,
you stood firm and gave me chance upon chance to be redeemed.
It was the gift that saved my life and loved me
back to the surface for new breath.
Your protection has allowed me to continually nurture
the gift even in the midst of confusion.

With every blow from evil you responded
with forgiveness, mercy and grace.
The gift of the new generation is essential
to the spiritual battle to come.

Preserving my life and my sanity for such a time
as this is but a piece of the journey.
You chose me and now the gift has been presented
back to you for a lifetime of service.

Empty Love

Kay Smith

Day to day I exist
Wondering how I missed
So much of life
Focused on love that never came
Now I am so far away
From anything concrete;
It's mundane
Just drifting higher
Until I expire
You say you loved me
Liar, liar

Beautiful Seed

Kay Smith

Ain't got no daddy here on earth
Momma never wanted me – no worth
Siblings disconnected
Relationships all busted – expected
Heart so torn, love so worn, soul forlorn
Sometimes I wish I'd never been born
Born alone, lived alone, died alone
But God... a beautiful seed sown
My gift from the throne

Biologically Abandoned

Kay Smith

My mother's womb was the start
from a donor unbeknownst to me
all I have are empty tales
from a missing history

No "DaVinci Code" to unlock the key
no human mind that knows
the only people that know all the parts
have gone on to eternally doze

To chase the past and find the truth
one must have all the clues
for me this has all proved for naught
for the start was all wrong news

The legal proof is false
the immoral proof is true
but there is no one still alive
to reconcile or construe

The search is always in my mind
of who this inoperative is
a futile, never ending search
with no answers to the quiz

I imagine that he wonders
and perhaps he even cares
and if my life would've been different
no twists, no turns, no flares

There will be no party
no welcome home my child
I don't even know that anyone has looked
perhaps I'm not worth the while

My mother's womb is now deceased
I'm all grown up as well
But the little child still longs to know
Where dost my father dwell

Hidden Agendas

Kay Smith

Nothing is right for me
Hidden agendas abound
Nowhere is safe to be
I seem to be bait for perverts
lost and found
It pains me to feel that grounds for
healthy relationships just aren't real
Define. I can't.
The guilt, the fault is mine
Ungodly I am, is it destiny
Close your eyes, try to find
the peace within, release your mind
Pervert, introvert, living hell
I feel death inside my shell
strangling me slowly
dayum what's left
Process. I can't.
Can't you tell
Hidden agendas
take the very life
I try to defend
Come out of that shell
Fix. I can't.
Safety is within.

Scene I

Kay Smith

A life of being disconnected
No one to call my own
Always ashamed of constant rejection
From birth til nearly grown
Born with a purpose
I'm not so sure
Underneath the surface
I'm not so pure
Constant violation
It started in the womb
With no consideration
That a life it would doom
Try to change how it ends
But the in-between
is the same as when it began
and – scene

Scene II

Kay Smith

Fightin' for my sanity – again
But, determined not to give in
Bad choices that I've made
Eventually I have to pay
Am feelin' alone in this misery
So thanks for your belief in me
Remove the option, make it so
Of the past I must let go
The ghost of her has been my bane
She lives rent-free in my insane
A continuous fight with shame and neglect
To control the game, I must expect
To win and live with no regrets
I can, I must, I cannot quit
It's all a game, it doesn't fit
I lost the round, I lost the fight
Been holding on with all my might
I wish I had just one good friend
That one someone I can depend
To cry, to lean and just detox
To help me think outside the box
and - scene

Searching

Kay Smith

I don't fault you for emotional neglect
you could never be and give what wasn't there
your job was an incubator, you gave me life
and I'm here; you did your job

All these years, my struggle has been you…
every friendship, every relationship, every
hurt, every pain, every choice
I looked for you; both of you
I could see you, but I never felt you; it was a mirage

My heart is so broken, in so many places
Life doesn't come with instructions
I have been so lost for pretty much all of it

God has seen fit to give me wisdom, yet I
am so dumb, so empty, so alone
I know HE loves me, but there seems to be nothing there to love
I just can't grasp anything

For so many years I stayed to me; it was safe
Now, I feel like I have lost my voice
Like everyone has the game plan, but me…

And I still have the same shattered heart
Searching for you…

Reflection on Rejection

Kay Smith

The rejection started in the womb…
Everyone has a bond…except me
I tried so hard to attach
somewhere, to something, to someone…
I hate it here, but here is where I am
I move from decade to decade, life to life
No one stays for very long
Trying to be helpful doesn't work
It only pushes people away
My first choice at love, at intimacy turned out to be so empty
I showed up; only to be misunderstood, used and then rejected
From there it just got worse; the saga continues…

Fear

Kay Smith

Fear comes in a variety of ways
It keeps you from sleeping
It wakes you up at night
It creeps in mid-day
It takes away your words and thoughts
making you blank and speechless
It floods your very being and guides your choices
It won't let you hear other voices… only noises

Be Free

Kay Smith

I pray that my bondage won't be your bondage
and my loneliness won't be your loneliness
I pray you will break through....and live

I see your struggle
I know your story
But you were put here
For HIS glory
Live your life son
For you were chosen
The devil knows this
And wants you dozing
When you come to you, it will be too late
An eternal hell will be your fate

I pray that my bondage won't be your bondage
And my loneliness won't be your loneliness
I pray you will break through.... And live

Truth

Kay Smith

Fatherless; Motherless - Friendless
Rejection, guilt and shame – endless
My thoughts are not facts – defend this
My Savior, my King – sinless

The Gift of Life and Choice - pt 2

Kay Smith

The gift continues to struggle…
Existing and searching
Wandering and hurting
Longing for that biological connection
We share the same complexity of rejection
Only heaven knows the pain and can erase the stain
of being conceived, but not received; how inane
Looking for a father, looking for a mother
Separation of time, but still no cover
The curse still hovers, though decades apart
Just emptiness and guilt for the two lonely hearts
I would give anything for the gift to be free
From the cruel and self- absorbed enemy
When will you realize the damage you've done
To the precious gift – your first born son
I long to see the final resolve
When the gift becomes free and learns to evolve
Coldness, darkness, total disdain
So insincere, it's completely insane
As I look back, I can only reflect
Why the choice was made to totally reject
An innocent life that had no voice
In where it was placed and had no choice
But to accept the chaos of awkward dysfunction
And try to survive with high hopes of conjunction
I look at the gift of life as it grows and its worth
And I long for the day of healing and spiritual re-birth
Returning to the creator from the ancient of days
From glory to glory in total praise

Replay

Kay Smith

I try to fit in, but I guess it's not my time
Always present, but not included, living in a hidden shine
So eccentric in character, but pure in heart
Patiently waiting for the dawn of a brand new start
Passed by again, silent pain
You smile and continue to play the game
Over and over, I run tape in my mind
I try to fit in, but I guess it's not my time….

Trapped inside with no idea why
Trying to reach out before I die
All I can do is speculate
Why no one can truly relate
I think of those that have come and gone
No effort to commit, no right or wrong
Over and over, I run tape in my mind
Only to see that I'm relationship blind…

Only God knows my heart and feels my pain
Only He can truly, truly sustain
Only God knows my fears and can make me free
He will be near to the broken hearted
He chose me

Destination

Kay Smith

I saw my past
And wondered why I ever dwelled there
Just endless pit stops with empty encounters

I'm in my present
Wondering how I got here
Just existing and hoping

I pray for the future
Wondering if I will arrive
free and able to live completely in YOU

Travelling to?

Kay Smith

I watch as everyone arrives to their destination in life…
I'm still on connecting flights
Destination – unknown.
Looking back…
There's nowhere to go back to
I never fit in to begin with
I long for the day when someone will really see me…
I fear it won't be until after death.

Heartbreak

Kay Smith

Broken hearted from the womb
Birthed into light, but dwelled in a tomb
Never connected, just passed along
Hoping to survive, fighting to stay strong
Scratching, clawing to make my way
Trying to flourish without decay
Fighting for every breath of air
Wishing and hoping that someone would care
Surface content, but not deeply within
Damaged and stained, but no earthly blend
Spiritual discernment, pleading heart
No understudy to play the part
Little girl grown, but still displaced
Little girl alone with memory erased
No familial connection, no place to call home
Except the space in my heart where the Savior roams
From creation to death lived the broken heart
But the Savior was there from the end to the start
Conceived in sin, but bathed in love
From a Father who chose me like hand into glove

Help!

Kay Smith

Falling apart is no joke.
It's even tougher when you're surrounded by people,
but not one single person helps you pick up one
single piece to help get you back on track......
Dayum it hurts.....help!

Burst

Kay Smith

I have to get my feelings out
Even though they're filled with pain
If I don't, my heart will burst
And I will cease to be....
Alone I entered.
Alone I dwelled.
Alone I'll exit.

Retreat

Kay Smith

Temporary acquaintances give false hope
and produce silence and withdrawal...
Retreat for survival.

Praise Team Bully

Kay Smith

Misunderstood at every turn
Lesson taught, lesson learned
Coming out of the comfort zone
So carefully built and maintained
Is totally a vendetta that cannot be explained
Placing blame, pointing fingers,
The sting of rejection continues to linger
Accusations, deep, deep hurt
Never valued, not much worth
You know my heart, you know my thoughts
Isolation will set in…
Misunderstood, misunderstood
Again and again and again….
Guidance, direction? Defeat.
Decision, decision; retreat.
Speechless, speechless; I keep...
Praying, praying for peace. but
No one can offer relief
From a praise team bully

Emotional Safety

Kay Smith

Scattered through decades, feelings of the unloved
No long-term connection from below or above
Hoping and yearning for just a glimpse
of relation, friend and other ships
Briefly looked at, never too deep
No one to invest, no true belief
Waking each day with new hope of being seen
But another lost day of mishaps and in-betweens
In-between spaces, people and places
In-between self, I can never embrace it
Emotional safety? There is none.
I keep on searching, but the pain has begun
Scattered, shattered and broken within
Rejected, neglected; how did this begin
Insecure, unsure, riddled with shame
The guilt of naiveté and believing the game
Emotional safety? Nowhere to be found.
Scattered through decades; still feeling bound
How do I let go, how do I proceed
My belief in my Father is all that I need
Lord, help me I cry; my life is all yours
Take it, use it and guide me to shore
To emotional safety and deep peace within
So, the decades of doubt will cease and come to an end

Disposable Me

Kay Smith

Disposable me. Discarded again.
Who is she? Left to fend
For daily survival from beginning to end
No one to reach out, no hand to lend

Who really sees into my being
Who remains and continues seeing
The true heart beating that gives and gives
The true heart beating that's afraid to live

Not really wanted, entered alone
Emotional connection never shown
Little girl lost without true friends
Little girl grown rejected again

There can never be another me, you only get one life
I just never got a chance to really be "un" disoposable and to rectify
Each time I'm let go from someone's space, I wonder what did I do
To be disposed of by man, not given a chance
to experience a love that's true

Disposable me. Crying in pain.
Hoping to see someone remain
And not flee the scene, but help to maintain
A life that's been passed by and consistently drained

Disposable me, but I'm breaking free
Re-entering the space that was made for me

Antisocial

Kay Smith

You say I am distant, standoffish, unapproachable
and not willing to mix with people;
So you label me and judge me, but you really don't know me
Passed by and overlooked for decades; walls begin to form, but
I watch and observe with a fierceness;
seeing where I can jump back in
See, I believe in my potential......can you
Self-actualization is at risk.

Disregard

Kay Smith

I didn't think about the feelings of a careless person
One that is being careless with others and
their feelings and well-being...
I showed disregard and for that I feel heaviness
No matter the circumstance or situation, no one deserves disregard
We are all flawed, we all make mistakes; we are human
Disregard is painful and denies existence
The least of these has a purpose, whether I see it or not
I have been the disregarded and so it's painful to realize
I am guilty; I didn't think...

Love...

Afraid

Kay Smith

The first time I saw you
I was afraid to hug you
The first time I hugged you
I was afraid to kiss you
The first time I kissed you
I was afraid to love you
The first time I loved you
I was afraid to lose you
The first time I lost you
I was afraid to move on
So I stayed and hoped
and you came back
it's been two more times since then
now I know I must move on
but…..
I'm afraid

On This Day

Kay Smith

On this day of sacred days
In this place of sacred places
You will become
my dearest
friend,
my love,
my partner
on a life journey

Intimacy

Kay Smith

Just a touch, a hug,
A hand held, an embrace
I don't know that anyone understands
You crave, long, yearn for these things
With such intensity….you'd
Almost die without it
It's not about them, it's about love
Intimacy

Relationships Awry

Kay Smith

I loved my mom
She loved me back - in her own way,
But I just couldn't feel it.

I loved my step dad
He loved me back – like another woman
I felt ashamed.

I loved my sister
She loved me back – it was twisted,
But she went away, I felt confused.

I loved my brother
He loved me back – like a little sister
And now he loves someone else.

I loved my ex
He loved me back for a while – it was all for sex
He left and now he loves someone else.

I loved my best friend
He says he loved me back
He ran away with my heart
Now I have no one that loves me
I'm starting over again…..I'll learn to love myself

Connection

Kay Smith

Our hearts are linked, our souls are connected
Our intimate love forever, our friendship respected
To water, to grow, to till, to know
My seed, my need
On your love to feed, only
I want so much the friendship to succeed
A healthy love is a rare breed that I want
To feel free to explore
Your inner most soul
Now and before
Your mind, your body
Complete – whole
Blooming, sweet blossom,
Nectar beneath
Enticing, calling
Please enter, don't retreat
Inquisitive, intimate, our hearts are linked

Ssshhhh

Kay Smith

Sometimes I listen to you talk and I just smile
Cause you say the sweetest things
Other times I listen to you talk and I crack up
Cause you are so goofy
Today I listened to you talk, with me, about you
And I fell even more in love with you, with our friendship
Sometimes I hear fear, pain and sorrow in your voice
Sometimes I hear tears, silent ones
Sometimes I hear frustration, confusion and despair
Other times I hear contentment and satisfaction
today I heard and felt so much, it was all so awesome
I listened and I heard and felt your love
Through all of these emotions
Its in those times that our love is being formed and our friendship laid
Its in those times that I come to know a part of you that
Otherwise I couldn't possibly know with just a physical relationship
Its in those times that we have become one
and know we are right for each other
Its in those times that I want you forever.......

Dilemma

Kay Smith

What is the dilemma?
I like tradition, but there is no tradition in my life right now
Old school is my heart, but not available
New school is a trend and very available
I crave its vibe, but in a pure sense
New school soothes temporarily
but leads to spiritual death.
It's not about new school,
it's about love, affection and safety
Plain and simple
Only, I was taught confusion. Period.
All the music, all the notes are
all jumbled on top of each other
when you pull them apart
they are fearful, not knowing who they are
I try to tune the station, but clarity is elusive…still I choose tradition.
I choose love.
What is the dilemma? I like tradition.
The dilemma is love

In Love

Kay Smith

Knowing, feeling
You feel so real, so right
Longing, wanting
Just to steal a moment
Just to hold you tight
To intrinsically be
The one to see
Your beauty and grace
The seductive sincerity
The smile on your face
The tone of your voice
Listen, listening
The words spoken
So soft, so moist
Knowing, feeling
You are the one
Hoping, perhaps doubting
What's to become
Will you, can you be there
Are you someone to trust
Someone to share
Their heart, their soul
This is a must
To fear your love, your physical touch
Yet, to yearn, to burn, this is such
Agony, pain, I can't explain
My love, my fear, my doubts,

Reservations
All turn into
Severe hesitations of
Knowing, doubting, feeling
Emotions that need healing
Just to be
Intrinsically free
Uninhibited in my love
The one to see
You and eventually
Perhaps even me

Forsaken

Kay Smith

Have you ever experienced love in its rawest form?
Pure and uninhibited by insecurities and doubts
Just the desire of complete satisfaction each time we meet
Our minds and hearts have already gone there
The final reality is the touch
from your soul to mine that
brings tears of contentment
I close my eyes and imagine being there
I smile, then sigh and wait
Darkness... void of touch
Words bring me back to the realization of you
with another
touching souls and bringing contentment
I am forsaken

Regrets

Kay Smith

I chose to let you in again
The reception was great, but
What have I done
It was all based on a moment, a feeling
I regret that.
I started to breathe you again
I was so hopeful.
The realization that change is constant stood still…
for you have not changed
All it took was one shot directly to the heart
I must now allow my maturity to work
I must decide.
Can my process take another hit?
Squeezed in
Can I be ok with being^ to your style?
Can I be ok with having infinite understanding?
Respect is missing / Respect is key.
What have I done?
In choosing you over pure air,
My breathing is now labored.
Therefore, I must now choose me and have
No regrets.

Twisted Love

Kay Smith

Look man, you have me twisted
So intense, I really miss it
Attention for me was so real
My whole heart you did steal
No room at the inn
Rejected again
I really believed
Our love could succeed
But along came the truth
Imparted by youth
Just a temporary thing
An encouraging fling
To jump start your race
And regain your place
I stand alone now
Wondering how
To move on and let go
From such a deadly blow
To my heart and my brain
And figure out how to cure my insane
Getting up from that gutter
And pump a heart with no flutter
No bosom to rest
No place to digest
Abandon, neglect
Anger, no respect
I see who you are
And even though sub par
I long for the feeling

That had me reeling
And took me away
And made me forget Kay
I am back to my place of pain
Trying to untwist and regain
What I lost in that maze
And no longer be dazed
By a false reality
that won't let me be
complete in my reason
and content with my season

Longing

Kay Smith

I look into your eyes
and I want to stay,
but I can't;
you aren't mine.
I stare and wish
that someone
would've been torn over me,
but no one was ever really there.
I look into your eyes again
and you're gone…
there's just a trail of mannequins
that take all of your time and energy
and never give back…bendable affection
it's not real love

Reality

Kay Smith

If I had your eyes to look into every time I felt hurt......
I would be bathed in love for eternity....
My reality is a mirror
And there....I drown in pain.

The Heaviness of Love

Kay Smith

Have you ever loved so intensely it consumes your very being
Your every thought, breath, and emotion over stimulates
You function, but every movement hurts
You try to move on, but your heart aches
It's not the first heart break; but it could be the last
No heart can continue to take this
Your tears are heavy with pain
You feel so ashamed, so alone, so confused
Why is your love so unwanted and so misunderstood
You're so naïve and stupid
The trail of relationships is never ending
it started at the thought of fornication
the only body being buried is mine; I can't breathe
my very first relationship just never quite took off; mother and child
and all the rest followed suit

Mature Love

Kay Smith

Mature love is uncomplicated; it sees the big picture
It is committed and nurturing; it cares for self and others
Mature love is rare; it loves you through the entire journey
It prayerfully keeps you lifted and celebrates you
There are no ill intentions; it's pure
It's not seasonal…

Seasons of Love

Kay Smith

Many cold spells have penetrated my heart in this lifetime
but your love warms me, it's a paradigm
As the cold winds blow and begin to numb my heart
Your love is there to comfort me and helps me to re-start
It thaws me out like the snow that's melting in spring
Peace, contentment and healing is what you're offering
But situation and circumstance can sometimes determine
The mood and the direction of the under current
Of my thoughts and emotions, I get lost in what I see
But your love covers all and lost in it is where I should be
With each day and daily prayer, I long to stay connected
To a sincere God that cares for me and makes me feel protected
The seasons of my life are all within your hand
You've given me hope and strength, you have the master plan

Influences...

Friend for Life

Kay Smith

Stately, regal, virtuous and wise
"For such a time as this" I realize
Royal heiress, child of the king
Daughter of wisdom among many things
Enemy of none, but target of Satan
Yes, the attacks are all definitely blatant
But, in all of the years your soul hasn't wavered
Like many before you by GOD you are favored
You study to lead
by faith you succeed
O daughter of Zion
iron does sharpen iron
Your focus has been – Women In Godly
Services, which shortened is WINGS
But you didn't stop there for there's Wingsters, Winglets and Twings
I marvel in awe at this woman of God
Who by Jesus himself has been given the nod
To saturate these women with the Word and HIS love
For the two go together just like hand into glove
From the book of James to our Passion Renewal
An example you've been and it hasn't been dual
For the fruit that you bear has been given by the slice
For everything you've accomplished has
been through obedience to Christ
The foundation has been laid for future generations
For all of those who will get the revelation
That nothing is right, holy, pure and divine
Unless Father, Son and Spirit are the light that shine
You have removed self, you use spiritual eyes
For you are truly – Stately, regal, virtuous and wise

Elegance, Grace and Beauty

Kay Smith

Elegance

I often look on in amazement at where our lives have taken us.
I've never really known you or your
background, your story so to speak,
but, as long as I have known you, you have remained the same.
We are so different, yet we are the same.
You have lived in small apartments and places of elegance,
But elegance is a state of mind, not just a state of being.
As I try to define you, I find only awe and admiration
as you help all that cross your path in big and small ways,
sharing what God has given to one so worthy.
You are in a league of your own.

Grace

There are people I have met and they were meant for a season,
But, all of my seasons have included you in some way.
Even when we drift because of the witness protection,
We pick up where we left off when you resurface.
You have always been most gracious with me, it is so effortless for you.
This gift that God has bestowed upon you is a wonder to be seen.
Your family is truly blessed to have such a gracious gem in you
as a daughter, sister, mother and wife.

Beauty

Never have I felt judged only respected and encouraged.
I have been at some pretty low points in my life,
Afraid to trust, afraid to live and even breathe;

not able to even look at people,
but, you were there even when you weren't, always checking in.
The beauty of this friendship is that you know
even though it's not in detail.
I could never thank you or repay you,
I just hope you know how special you have been to me.
I watch and observe even when you are not aware
And you always amaze me.
To peel away your layers and find pain and disappointment
Would only be for a fleeting moment
Because these things will forever be out layered by
your elegance, grace and beauty

Great is Thy Faithfulness

Kay Smith

You have been faithful over a few things
HE will make you ruler over many
for you have been encouraging to all
but devoted to HIM
Great is thy faithfulness

Your countenance is angelic
You have truly been slow to anger
Remaining constant and steadfast
faithful to all
Great is thy faithfulness

You were determined not to be in bondage
to the choices of the past
with boldness, sincerity and faith
that HE would sustain; a testimony was given
Great is thy faithfulness

You truly are a class act through Christ
You are on the wall for the kingdom
Your light is a beacon for all to see
Good and faithful servant
Great is thy faithfulness

Trusting the Process

Kay Smith

I look back and visit many conversations
Kids…school…marriage…dreams…goals…salvation…life
Through it all we've come to realize
there's a process to life.

Time is a funny thing
It can tick by slowly
or escape you completely,
it's a process.

You have been a part of my life
for what seems like a very long time
only….so much has escaped us,
it's a process.

There's always something left unsaid
or some project left undone…
our children are grown; where have the days gone?
It's a process.

The one constant thing
that has become of us
is you leading me by example to
trust the process.

I have come to value those words
and share them with others
it truly is wisdom at it's best
and through it all I've come to realize that
ultimately, the process is Christ.
Thank you for instilling the love of the process in me…..

Journey of the Designated Homeless

Kay Smith

You opened your home to one who had none.
There were no second thoughts or hesitation.
Generosity was the norm.
Designated or not;
home is a state of mind.

A home is a place of connection and memories;
a haven for the brokenhearted to heal.
Security, safety and peace should be the norm.
Love and Christian principles should dwell therein.
Peace is a state of mind.

I have been in a homeless state all of my life;
there was no connection, safety, security and no peace.
The norm was survival.
Love was twisted and scarce; life was combat.
Survival was a state of mind.

I will have memories of the home that physically was not mine;
in my mind I was safe, secure and cared for.
Christian principles were the norm.
Love was abundant and free.
Freedom is a state of mind.

Home is a journey
for those that are
designated homeless.
Their connections and memories are transient;
as is their state of mind.

The Day God Orchestrated Just For Me

Kay Smith

I started not to go; I had so much to do,
But GOD took care of that, for HE already knew.
The word was spoken and it was just for me
The message was patience and forgiveness; forgiveness is key.
From the worship songs to the skit and ending with the word
most definitely let me know that the prayers had been heard.
A meal shared in faith and a testimony received
put Satan on notice that he did not succeed.
The saints were on watch, they were up on that wall
we were lifted in prayer and they didn't let us fall.
One of the vessels GOD used had on spiritual eyes,
for He knew that the faith of my son was indeed the prize.
September the tenth of 2006 will be a day I will share
that someone took the time and for me they did care.
The story continues and has yet neared the end
But I'm confident in CHRIST that HIS people will win.
From beginning to end GOD made his point
in choosing the people that HE did anoint
to aid in the day that was orchestrated for me
because HE knows what we need while we're on our journey.

The Leak

Kay Smith

What started as a trickle, became Niagara Falls
My life will never be the same, but I am standing tall
What Satan meant for damage, GOD has brought release
from isolation and seclusion, HE has restored the peace
That leak delivered me from being so unsure
to knowing that GOD'S love for me is steadfast and pure
I didn't understand the profoundness of this leak
until it rendered me homeless without a place to sleep
In being in this state, not sure of where to go
I asked the LORD to show me just what I didn't know
The vessels that HE used to bring this point full blown
reiterated what I knew and made the unknown known
HE doesn't want you wandering, lost, dazed and confused
HE wants to bring you unto HIM so that you can be used
The leak that started just as that brought bondage to the light
and educated me spiritually and made a struggle right
To be shoved out of your womb not knowing where you're going
Is equivalent to CHRIST coming to earth which is so mind-blowing
The FATHER loved me so much that HIS son HE gave
To die an excruciating and horrendous death so that I might be saved
What started as a ministry when Jesus came to earth
was really a divine plan from HIS death to life to birth
and so it is with the leak that started as a trickle
and soon became Niagara Falls and made my life so fickle
Life as I know it just will not be the same
for what Satan thought would take me out has made me up my game
I will be delivered, I will have my crown
the leak has served its purpose, the walls are tumbling down
If your life is leaking and you don't know what to do
Trust in GOD almighty HE will bring you through

The Voice Lesson

Kay Smith

The melodies of many who have gone before you
are all wrapped up in your soul as are those to come.
I close my eyes and I listen to them all.
I hear your father on his guitar singing, head slightly tilted.
I hear your mentor challenging your soul.
I hear the ancestors of your ancestors
encouraging and cheering you on.
They praise the day and time that you came into you.
They acknowledged as you fine-tuned, tweaked and prayed your way
into the lives of so many others.
Through you, comes the encouragement,
prodding and stretching of our God given talents.
The many who have experienced a season with you – celebrate,
for they now have new melodies in their souls.
Rema, I am but another of your melodies...
I thank you for hearing the music in me.

Crossing the Street

Kay Smith

You saw a fragile and fearful child;
afraid of touch, afraid of eye contact,
afraid to speak; and yes, afraid of life itself.
The child stood on one side and stared "beyond" for safety.
You stood on the other side and stared "at" in disbelief;
wondering how to get this child across the street.
You had hope and you cared; time and patience you surmised
would be the key to begin the journey.
As a crossing guard motioning that it's safe to venture out;
likewise, was your plan.
The child was frozen in the midst of the traffic, but you went out
and there you stood until the child was ready.
The traffic never made contact, you made sure of that.
Eventually, the child began to grow and made
attempts at crossing the street.
You waited and made sure the journey was safe.
Days, weeks, months and years have come and gone.
The child has finally come to terms with crossing the street.
Your plan was successful and slowly you faded.....and the child?
She looked you right in the eye and she flew...
right into your heart and your life,
but, over the traffic and into a life of her own.

The Gift

Kay Smith

When my mother passed,
you were there...silently praying and guiding me,
helping me to raise my son.

When my life fell completely apart
you were there...constantly checking on me and my spirit,
allowing me time to grieve and heal from all the failures.

When my spiritual walk was being shredded beyond belief,
you were there...sharing my pain and anger,
but never letting me dwell in that place.

You have been such a part of me for what seems like forever.
My awe for your character, wisdom and knowledge is beyond words.
You give new meaning to the word class and
integrity oozes from your soul.

Never have I heard one person speak negatively about you.
You are the exemplary spirit of Christ, a true woman of God;
going about your "Father's business" effortlessly.

When my mother passed, my life fell apart and
my spiritual walk was challenged...
you were there and it was effortless.
Thank you.

Falsely Accused

Kay Smith

I think of the hurt
and misunderstanding
I think of a friend I just adored
Never would I
come incorrect at you
or disrespect you
You were allowed
To look into my soul,
To see and know me
I don't understand
How you didn't know
That my true feelings
Were healthy…always
I never recovered from that accusation

ReeRee's Groove

Kay Smith

Do you know your ABC's?
Breathe in, breathe out,
ready, ready, go.
A,b,c,d,e,f,g,l,m,n,o,p…
I thought you knew you're A,B,C's,
let's try again once more.

Solfeggio syllables up and down
is movement for your soul
Do, ti, la, sol, fa, sol, la, fa, fa, mi, re, re, do
Drop your jaw, project your voice,
Ready, ready, go
Are you singing? I can't hear you.
Give me a little more
Do, re, do; mi, fa, mi; sol, sol, sol, sol, sol.
You can do it…I promise
Ready, ready, go

How are you doing with your song?
What's that face about?
You're going flat and between the notes.
Okay, let's work this out.
Take a good breath and
know what you want to do
The song has to be believable
for the audience and for you.

The scales and drills are preparing you
So keep working on that part;
remember to breathe, relax your jaw
and sing it from the heart.
You are a musician,
your instrument is your voice
so use your gift and sing out loud
make a joyful noise – rejoice!

Do you know you're A,B,C's?
Ready, ready, go...........
Do, ti, la, sol, fa, sol, la, fa, fa, mi, re, re, do.

Portrait of Negativity

Kay Smith

I listen to you and I hear it…
slowly seeping out of your soul
it is ever so subtle, but it's there.
Funny….I never heard it before.

It's the tone in your responses
and the choice of your words.
Sometimes you catch yourself,
But it hovers 'round about you.
Funny…I never caught it before.

I wonder when it came to be and why…
Doubt? Insecurity? Fatigue?
Or…perhaps the feeling that life has passed you by
and you don't know where to jump back in at.
I do understand, but
Funny…I never saw you <u>not</u> jumping back in.

How can I help? What can I do?
I hear frustration and regret
masked by "I'm okay, it will pass."
I hear impatience and empty inquiries
as to "when will it be my time."
I see the repetitive motions of a daily routine
occasionally splashed with a dash of joy.
Funny…I always saw joy as a constant variable for you.

Your life has been anointed
and many great things are to come
Only…there is no room for the negativity.
I pray for renewed inspiration in your spirit,
new direction for your life
and a back drop of joy with
not even one splash of negativity.
Funny…how our lives change,
but I never saw you <u>not</u> in the game.

Feet in My Back

Kay Smith

Gentle pressure from the Savior
through vessels here on earth
Anointing, vision, shifting to spiritual rebirth
Opportunities are here to bring honor to your name
Consuming fire deep within your passion we proclaim
The journey to the heart of God has been so insecure
I can't obtain my peace of mind for a love that is so pure
The gentle pressure is two feet in the small of my back
From a Savior who truly loves me and is keeping me on track
The vessels He is using to guide me safely through
Is to get to the me inside to get safely through to You
I must trust Him and believe Him to accomplish prophecy
And embrace the gentle pressure of those two most sovereign feet
The vessels that he sent to me are nudging me along
To a shine that's been waiting, but it seems so far beyond
The reality I've come to know within my comfort zone
But I know He won't forsake me or leave me all alone
Gentle pressure, gentle Savior, gentle vessels worth
The work it takes to get me to my spiritual rebirth

Fetish

Kay Smith

Balloons, socks and candy…
Symbolized closure,
Created growth
And opened doors…thank you

Jane Elliott

Kay Smith

Brown eyes, blue eyes; 1968
Assassination of a dream, different time; different place
But, is it really; we're all still toiling
Fifty years later, tempers are still boiling
White privilege, prejudice and discrimination
We're back where we started; breakdown in communication
We seem to forget that we all come from one place
The womb of a woman despite the melanin in our face
The sun-kissed skin that makes so many afraid
Bleeds the same red on the inside when at rest we are laid
Same bones, same organs, same fingers and toes
So why does dark skin make people your foe
Turning a blind eye to mistreatment of color
Will you reap what you sow as you stay undercover
The names of so many gone way too soon
The eye of the storm, we've learned nothing new
Sandra, Tamir, Philando and Trayvon
Mike Brown, Walter Scott, Oscar Grant and so on
Gunned down, choked out and mysterious deaths
Church shooting of nine and you're treated with respect
Social experiment – how did it feel
To find out bigotry is certainly real
To pretend you don't see it is such a disgrace
For we are all connected, it's called the human race

Change Maker
- Prophecy

Kay Smith

It's all about being concrete; don't worry, I got your back
I'll fight and stay the course until it fades to black

The passion for sincere change and to be the one
To care for those that have been overlooked and have come undone

Standing on the corners in your neighborhoods
Your goal is to try and understand those that are misunderstood

Seeking out ways to give back and to give them hope
is where you excel and you belong, for they need ways to cope

Making the decision to let go and return to being free
To follow the plan that was made for you to return to your reality

The gifts you were given to give honor to Him
will continue to manifest
For the King of Kings has given you favor,
you have been infinitely blessed

So, I accept the path He has for you, He doesn't make mistakes
For your life has been anointed from birth,
a change maker is what it takes

Healing

Kay Smith

I watch and observe her, she is unique
An odd duck of sorts, she says
Be bigger, better in your sleep
Define your thoughts, the past don't keep
Let your mind dwell on the good and positive things
that the future holds and that the future will bring
Be encouraged, you are doing great
Don't give up, this abuse is not your fate
Give yourself the time you need to heal
and you will succeed over all the perverse and wicked deeds
that were done in the dark, but have come to the light
in the mind of a woman that was once childlike
As I journey on to higher heights
I will not forget the odd duck of sorts that helped me to fight
and regain what's left of my spirit, soul and life.

Growth...

Growth

Kay Smith

I've grown with myself into myself
And I know I am not by my self
Because I've grown.

Processing Confusion

Kay Smith

Dormant pangs are beneath a fragile surface
suspended, but capable of arousal, longing to be alive
in a complete and wholesome way.
Entwined in the past,
Existing in the present,
Confused about the future.
Inside, deep inside, is the truth,
but, the very life is being choked from it
until….an exhausted surrender is inevitable.
Weary from the fight, truth is terminated.
Inside, deep inside, are the dormant pangs
and slowly they emerge, amoral, hungry and threatening
until…therapy processes
the past into the present and
squashes it for the future.
Dormant pangs are now
ashes to ashes and dust to dust.
Growth is inevitable.

GIT!!

Kay Smith

Girl you betta git outa my face!
Cause that's just how I'm feelin' today
You just don't know
What I'm in the process of
processing as we speak
You keep playin' games and
just straight trippin'
whiles I'm on my journey
Ima need you to just
bring it down a notch cause
I have no time for your trip
I'm taking my own
Girl, I'm goin' through myself
to myself
so Ima need you to give me some space
for myself
deal wit it and
git outa my face!
Holla!

Closing My Eyes

Kay Smith

I close my eyes to think – thoroughly
I close my eyes to see – the path
I close my eyes to remember – me
I close my eyes to forget – them
I close my eyes to feel safe – here
I close my eyes to hear – clarity
I close my eyes to imagine – peace
I close my eyes to – live
I close my eyes to – survive

Humorous Survival

Kay Smith

I laugh for sanity
Without my sense of humor
I am insane
and death is inevitable
I laugh for safety
Without my sense of humor
I am unsafe
And life is difficult
I crack myself up to survive

Conversation

Kay Smith

I want to be with you, to lay with you
I promise I won't hurt you, I will only love you
the way you were meant to be loved

I am not trying to be loved with a twist
I am trying to recover from being loved
the way someone else thought I should be loved
Being loved that way is too painful

Well I think you're beautiful
I like your smile, I like your laugh
I'd like to show you your beauty
If only you could see what I see

Silence....sigh
Thank you for all of your kind words
I am not able to receive the things you want to give
I have been dead to love for many years now
I cannot see what you see

Why are you so afraid of letting go?
Why do you fear people?
Why do you isolate yourself?
You have so much to offer.
It's time to allow yourself to be truly loved.

I cannot control others.
I cannot even control me.
People are hurtful.
Isolation is safety.
My time has not come yet for true love.

You're judging me based on your past.
That's not fair, I'm not like them.
Why won't you let me in?

I judge not, I am protecting me from my past.
Life is not fair, I don't know what you're capable of
I'm not like them either, but I'm also not like you
I can't have company today.

Visualize

Kay Smith

I close my eyes to visualize no pain
What does it look like to be pain free?
All I see is day to day
existence and survival
Clear it.

I close my eyes to visualize no pain
I see days of being bondage free
Able to control my thoughts
Instead of my thoughts controlling me
Claim it.

I close my eyes to visualize no pain
What do I want?
To sleep peacefully and
be free from painful dreams
Believe it.

I close my eyes to visualize no pain
Where will I be?
In a safe place, in a safe space
Within my heart, my mind and soul
Realize it.

I close my eyes to visualize no pain
What will I do?
I will remember, be ok with it
and know that I was not at fault
and that at any given point
I can close my eyes to
clear it, claim it, believe it, realize it
and visualize no pain.

I close my eyes to see my destiny
Pain free........

Nail Biting

Kay Smith

I trim so precisely until I see no more
It's as if I am trimming my life
In to this neat lil box
I can't seem to stop
I am down to the quick
And I am still trying to trim
It's painful at first
The bearing of the quick
But now the skin has hardened
I am left with a mess
What am I trying to expose?
I stare in disbelief
I am back at an old place
from my childhood
It's time for new growth

Being First

Kay Smith

My whole life I've waited my turn
In so many different lines
For so many different reasons
Just for a chance to be first to someone
empty promises have come and gone
I am still in line, waiting my turn
Kids come first. Don't they?
I was a kid, but my turn never came.
Family comes first. Right?
I had a family, I am still waiting.
What about a wife or a friend?
Do they come first sometimes?
These lines have unbearable wait times.
I try so hard, but no one notices
I have never progressed
to being first in any of those lines
so… I began to put others first
just to make the wait a lil more bearable
everyone has made it to the front of my line
I have managed to put everyone first
Except for me
I am still standing
in so many different lines
waiting my turn
when will the love of and for self kick in?
There are no lines when you are first to you.
Step right up, you can have a turn here
as often as you like

No Pain

Kay Smith

What is on the other side waiting there for me?
I'm so afraid to let go and experience being free
Holding on to the past has been my saving grace
So letting go at this point what will that erase?
The abuse has been a part of me locked inside this vault
Why can't I forgive myself it must've been my fault
Why were there no loving arms for this was I miscast?
Why could no one nurture me, I must have
been the difficulty from the past
Now that I am all grown up with baggage left to claim
I still cannot eradicate the pain, the guilt and shame
I want to be transformed from extraordinary hopelessness
to being internally cured
and my emotional and spiritual state I want to be assured
I have been operating on fumes not running on fuel
The ups and downs of doing that has torn me into dual
personalities unable to face reality and keeping me so bound
into confusion of the worst kind, it's all been so profound
I am so angry to say the least that myself I cannot find
It just takes so much detailed work to leave the past behind
What is on the other side waiting there for me?
I'm not so sure, but I finally need to just
let go and experience being free.

Surrender, Stand Back and See

Kay Smith

To surrender you must have faith
To have faith you must trust
To trust you must have a foundation
To have a foundation it has to be laid
To lay a foundation takes planning
To plan you must have goals
To have goals you must have a vision
To have a vision you must dream
To dream you must have hope
To have hope you must have Christ
To have Christ you must believe
In believing in Him you must surrender
To surrender to Him you must have faith.....

Oh child of God, stand back and see; we must surrender all
What challenges us is no test for Him; He's waiting for your call
The faith, trust and foundation that is being laid
was given to us long ago, for with His life He paid
The Father's goal for your life that was once conceived
was the plan of salvation so that we would believe
I'm sure that He envisioned a universe so free
from bondage, guilt, shame and sin far as the eye could see
In dealing with this human man the dream He had for us
was that our hope would be built on Him
and that would be enough
Oh child of God, stand back and see
As your walk with Him begins
and no matter the level of your faith
surrender and you will win

Small Things

Kay Smith

Reflecting back on where I've been and all that I've gone through
It's been the small things that have enabled me to renew
I have my sense of sanity on a daily basis
Cheering me on and providing me with constant oasis
I'm also grateful for being able to work even
though circumstances aren't the best
For learning how to lean on my faith during this, my life's test
For every period of my life when my mental state is consumed
With thoughts of I can't do this, I give up,
my faith keeps me from my tomb
I'm grateful for my son who lights up my every day,
his smile, his heart and sense of self has helped me pave my way
I'm grateful for my journey as painful as it's been
For it made me who I am external and within
I'm grateful for my health, my strength, my vision to believe
that I can one day began to heal, recover and achieve
all that I have been robbed of from so very early on
and that I can cease to exist and begin to
live and not be so withdrawn
Pat says I have so much strength that I just fail to see
and so I am grateful for knowing her and that in me she believes
but most of all I am just so very grateful for having life
so many times I should have died, but I'm
still standing through all the strife
So many small things have kept me like music, candles and soap
For these small things I am grateful for they
have been my saving grace and hope

Reflecting back on all the seasons of just being me
can make the small things into big and give the victory
and so I will continue to count my many blessings
and all my layers of issues I will keep addressing
for as the world proceeds to bling and keep on livin' large
the small things I appreciate will always be my charge

Letting Go

Kay Smith

You try so hard to attach, to belong
It always seems to turn out wrong
So you retreat, redefine and rebuild
The lessons are hard,
but you must swallow the pill
I am no better, but I am no less
I have a servant's heart
Is it all a test?

You were supposed to protect me
You never even attempted
By Satan this was all pre-empted
To steal my heart, mind and soul
To mar my very existence by all that he stole
I will never understand your pangs from the past
for you never shared your life, I have no contrast
Of the good, of the bad, the ups nor the downs
I'm not even sure I was wanted around
We shared a living space, but dared not to feel
any emotion, it was all so surreal

So in trying to attach, you become detached
And still all the time trying to latch
On to people, situations, material things
Yet the bad part is all the baggage it brings
I have to learn to belong to me

There is no price, no charge, my self love is free
My retreat has turned into redefinition
And as I rebuild I am on a mission
To mar the presence of Satan in my life
And continue to choose to do what's right
To let go of his agenda and all of his stuff
and to let him know that I've had enough

The goal is to focus, persevere and endure
To be forgiven and to forgive of this I am sure
I will no longer attach, I will no longer belong
To all of the things that have turned out wrong
My reconstruction will continue
for I now know that there are other choices on the menu
So enjoying all that Christ has for me
Is the future, the past is history.

Bondage

Kay Smith

You live your life, you never deal,
but I'm here to tell you, all the demons, they're real
You can persevere as you fight your fight
But hold your head up, for you are the light
you must let go of all that is wrong
to live your life to get your praise on
get rid of that stuff, no matter the struggle
no matter how tough, let it go on the double
I listen to the word, I try to receive
my day has to come, I have to believe
The sacrifice was made for me so long ago
up on that cross so my chance I can't blow
But the demons of life, they won't let you rest
yet though they slay me, I'll still do my best
To represent the kingdom and use His word
to put on the armor as I've so often heard
I want to live my life like Psalm 27
though mother and father forsake me, I have my Father in heaven
For this has been my bondage that has kept me locked on this isle
The feeling of being a motherless child
Not able to receive hugs, not able to receive love
Not even from my heavenly Father above
My journey is mine whether I claim it or not
I can take it and face it or expect the onslaught
of Satan's old tricks to punk me into shame
But the victory is mine, there's power in my game
And so I continue like others before me
To fight the good fight and give Him the glory
For saving a wretched wretch from utter confusion

Pain, guilt and shame, isolation and seclusion
My story could be yours cause we all have one to tell
because we or someone we know has been through a living hell
but I'm here today as a living witness and survivor
that God is a mother, father and yes, a provider
So if this is you or another child of God
Keep praying and believing, you will beat the odds
Don't let the fog keep you from the shore
Don't just exist, receive what God has in store
Don't ever give up, no matter how long it takes
hold on to your faith and the cycle will break

Point of Separation

Kay Smith

It's all been leading up to the point of separation
All the words, thoughts and all the conversation
The experience has been filled with much anxiety and pain
Storm filled nights with unrelenting rain
I listen with such intensity, hoping for a phrase
that would bring some clarity and release me from my maze
processing and processing, sure to be thorough
digging and delving into my system of neuro
it's time to let go, it's time to move on
for this has been the strategy of the
rook, knight and pawn
we went in
with similar feelings,
you saw so much pain
and I needed healing
for you touched and I crumbled from all of the "stuff"
that has held me in such bondage; Lord knows it's been tough
But for one little girl who was invisible to most
The journey to womanhood has been the riposte
Dormant I lay until I could fight to get beyond
And return to myself like the prodigal son
To welcome myself back into life as it seems
To nurture and foster my own self-esteem
I struggle to hold on, you're determined to be free
So I must let go and learn to "do me"
I'm definitely at odds and yes I'm afraid,
But I know I've evolved from the impact you've made
I cry at the thought of going it alone
But the point of separation is yet another milestone

So as we prepare to go our separate ways
In the upcoming months, weeks or perhaps even days
I will take your belief in me and come out from within
Because I've begun a war that I expect to win

Alive But Bound

Kay Smith

The voice of creation spoke
and life consumed the lifeless;
he took breath, but he was bound.

When he came forth from the grave
from the sleep of a life time;
he moved, but he was bound.

As he shook off death to proceed to life
he became free, one step at a time;
Lazarus was no longer bound.

The struggle for me began before time
before my conception;
I took breath, and came here bound.

Speak life into me oh Father divine
I exist, but I do not live;
I am here, yet I am bound.

The layers of life smother and hang about me
like the grave clothes of death;
I hope, yet I am bound.

The test of faith stretches my essence
as it did for my lineage;
I pray, yet I am bound.

As I take mental rest from the business of life
and heal, grow and mature;
I shed existence and begin to live.

The voice of creation spoke
and delivered me from me;
I am no longer bound.

I AM NO LONGER BOUND.

It's Not About Me

Kay Smith

Girl, don't you know the plan? It's not about you and me.
God doesn't want you dead in sin, He wants you to be free.
He gave his son to the world, so that He would be glorified,
He shook his head and wept for us, as his only son did die.
God gave his son to make the point so that we might believe,
so don't get it twisted it's all about Him; not you and no not me.
You are the vessel that He chose to carry the plan through,
your soul was lost and so He came to strengthen and renew.
You walk around thinking that around you the world does turn,
wake up girl and pay attention; you've got a lot to learn.
Who are you that you think the kingdom won't advance
because you didn't use your gift or give the saints a chance?
Christians are not perfect; they're not even close,
that's why HE died up on that cross, the world was comatose.
He wants to do it with us, but if He's not received,
He'll take his spirit from us and by the world we'll be deceived.
The second chance that we have to work the plan divine
should be our whole agenda, for it's not our will but thine.
The next time Satan creeps in and wants
to make this thing about you,
check yourself, talk to God, it seems you're overdue.

Pressing

Kay Smith

My faith in you
Keeps me going
I just don't know where
you're taking me
I've taken so many trips
without you
but you've helped me to
survive each one
I'm battered
but I'm still standing
and you
keep fighting for me
I can't let go
I can't give up
but, I'm so lost
In emptiness.....

But God

Kay Smith

I am overwhelmed by transition
and emotionally overcome by change.
There's so many decisions to be made
and so much work to do.
There are so many people to guide
and so many people to answer to.
Where am I in the midst of it all?
Who am I?
Am I being herded along as cattle or
am I making choices?
Choose this day whom you will serve!
For the time and choice will surely pass…
The banks of the mind, heart, soul and spirit are flooded
with "what ifs and should of, would of, could ofs…"
The world has gone mad and hope seems dim.
BUT GOD…
HE ALONE…
Regulates, motivates, and captivates;
inspires greatness and makes me aspire for greatness;
soothes, calms and brings peace and tranquility;
heals and mends my shattered spirit;
insures, ensures, and assures;
provides, protects, and secures the insecure;
gives strength to the weak and timid;
makes fences to give protection to the unprotected;

brings tears to a heart of stone;
gently nudges the unforgiving into a state of forgiveness;
shows himself faithful to those who lose their faith;
is hope to those in a state of despair;
gives hugs to those that are not open to them; and
JUST LOVES A MESS LIKE ME
BUT GOD...

Nail it to the Cross

Kay Smith

I look at the cross, I envision my life
I see all the blood covering me
If it had not been for this selfless act
where and who would I be

My Jesus, my Savior, my Redeemer and King
was beaten and nailed to that cross
this sacrifice He made just for me
was my wretched life worth the cost

Apparently so because that's just what He did
that my soul would forever live
He hung, bled and died, but rose again
and asked His Father to forgive

The cross represents so much for me
It's been my saving grace
Seventy times seven and one by one
all my sins the blood did erase

As I look back at my life and all that I've done
the guilt, shame, and baggage galore
I think, what can I do to honor my King
that has helped me survive and restore

I will take all that mess that has had me so bound
and examine and begin to exhaust
all that is not like Christ and beneficial to me
and I will simply just nail it all to the cross

Moving On

Kay Smith

How do you know when it's time to move on?
I can't explain it, it's just the feeling…
The feeling of being alone inside and out
You reach for familiarity
only things have become unfamiliar
Your comfort zones are uncomfortable
and the people in your life
are sending you messages
some subtle and some blaring
but nonetheless messages that
it's your time to let go
You are not ready, but it takes two
So…you gracefully bow out
and nervously attempt
to enter into a new time of your own
you ponder your next move,
breathe in the moment
and the unexplainable feeling
that you now know it's your time to move on.

Reaping

Kay Smith

You say, now you understand the hurt you've caused
Someone has done the deed to you
You want my support as you sift through the ashes
To be honest – I don't want to help you with your pain
But, I will make this a teachable moment in time for you…
Oh, and by the way…you're very welcome

Half of 114

Kay Smith

My life has been a puzzle with many missing pieces
To find one is to lose one, my search; it never ceases
Searching off and on in fear; afraid of everything
I can't believe it's still unclear; I'm half of 114.

It's like, I see the pieces hovering 'round about my space,
But I reach out to assemble them, but the fear I can't erase
God has a plan for everything and all the pieces to the puzzle
And even at half of 114, He sifts through all my rubble

He molds me and restores my strength to make my life complete
He loves me back to see myself as He has always seen
From the long-lost little girl that suffered in defeat
And respectfully restores my life at half of 114.
The journey continues………

Expectations...

Kay Smith

Real or imagined...shallow
Mine are intense because of past pain...fallow
The list continues to grow into desperation for basic human need
That no one can meet and I must concede
To a new approach...one of belief, trust, love
Not from below, but only above
If I can let go of here, I can move to over there
To a goodness of fit where nothing can compare
I must commit to the expectation of me
to be completely at peace and ultimately set free
From a place where others misconstrue my intent
Real or imagined, I cannot invent
Shallow expectations... imagined or real
My expectation is to finally heal
From buying in to all the hype
And letting it be in control of my life
To be in such bondage from the mess of others
Is to become a toxic dump and continue to smother
The expectations I have of me and to lure
Things from darkness that are definitely impure
I can't control you and I can't control me
Control comes from my Father and He
Alone is the lifter of my head
And I believe Him when He said
I am fearfully and wonderfully made
So the expectation is to live up to the price He paid
For a lost and wretched soul that was so hell bound
Until He came and broke up fallow ground
No longer a victim of worldly strangulation
To be one with Him that's my expectation

Identity

Kay Smith

The best me? Who is she?
Lost, but found and now I see
So much confusion and deep regret
I have so much pain to let go of yet
I self-reflect to make it through
Internal narrative must be new
Swirling thoughts of being free
No crushing bondage for eternity
Digging deep to find the root
To pull it out is my pursuit
To find a way to heal the pain
And unleash the grudge of deep disdain
My prayer is that I break the mold
Of generational stuff from centuries old
My father - invisible, my - mother bitter
My siblings - lost, but I must consider
Where I'm going, where I've been
Stuck on repeat, what's happening
To my progress to see my shine
I can't give up, it's now my time
I cannot let it pass me by
And continue to keep on asking why
Why me? Why not me?
Unleash my thoughts and let me be
The daughter you created for your glory
To trust you God is mandatory
For my deliverance; end of story
The best me? Who is she?
Daughter of the King's identity

Trippin'

Kay Smith

I'm so tired of being misunderstood
Taken for granted since the days of childhood
Over and over made to feel less
Than other people at their worst or their best
Am I just the safe target that these people need
So they assume and attack; on my kindness they feed
After all of my work on me has been devoured
My insides and outsides completely scoured
I am left with a carcass, an unidentifiable mess
To try and rebuild, renew and re-invest
Hurting people; hurt people
Some do it on purpose
To knock you out of the game
So you never re-surface
All these people trippin' on their own mess
Can throw a wrench into my success
But putting on the armor of my Christ and my King
Protects and restores me to bring
The best that I am to the daily grind
To press on, persevere and renew my mind
I am a child of thee most high; I give honor and praise
To the one who protects me from your hurtful ways
So keep on trippin' all you want
I'm in ghost mode; you cannot haunt
You cannot creep, stalk or even kill
For the strength inside of me is real
I will continue to stay on the path He has laid
And excuse myself from your game of charades

Lost, But Found

Kay Smith

Never ending journey to know who I am; its been years
Deep down inside I tremble with fear
I try and I try, but I can't shake it loose
I cry and I cry, I can't fake it, what's the use
I search with a fierceness trying to visualize
The meaning of me; yet it's always minimized
I see darkness, I see nothing, but I see perfectly clear
That there may be no tomorrow, will I live to be here
Very early on I wanted to be – alive
But fighting each day to merely survive
Became the game of who will I be today
To get through safely, but never being Kay
No direction to a final destination
All I have is a misguided connotation
Lost in abuse, confusion and shame
Totally mocking the meaning of my name
Kay means pure, how can this be
For every wicked thing was done unto me
Closing my eyes to imagine it gone
Just wishing for somewhere that I could belong
Always pretending; chameleon extraordinaire
Giving up me for someone who cares
Not understanding, not knowing the real value of me
Even though conceived in sin, I was meant to be free
The God of creation and giver of life
Never gave up on me and continued to fight
To get me to a place of being content
And in each situation to forgive and repent
Never ending journey to know who I am; continues
Chosen by Yahweh; new venue

40 Plays in 4 Days

Kay Smith

Fearful of people, but determined to grow
Struggling with it, but I had to let go
Creativity deep down within
Taking the long way to refresh and begin
On a journey of prophecy from long ago
To begin to fulfill and make it so
Battling rejection and the need to withdraw
It took deep reflection to not let it gnaw
And fester beneath my calm exterior
But the faithful few never once let me feel inferior
Stand for what's right or let your silence speak
Volumes upon volumes and render you weak
I have to pick and choose my battles and stay true to me
My response can't harm others, I need to be free
Of lashing out when I know I'm at peace
Don't play a part, the madness must cease
The 40 plays in 4 days was a test of my faith in my Father
That no matter the trial or situation, ill will He won't let me harbor
The true reason for the trip was not about
me and it wasn't about the crew
It was about all the gifts He instilled in each
one and networking to give us all new
New vision, new thoughts and new life for
the part that we play in His story
To stay on the wall and answer the call to

be all that we can for His glory
So as I look back on satan's attack to tear it all apart
God really stepped in and did not let rejection seep into my heart
I will continue to work on the struggle and
continue to give Him the praise
And not let the trick of the enemy prevent
the lesson of 40 plays in 4 days

The Big Picture

Kay Smith

I didn't conceive or even believe
That a word spoken would one day come true
But now that I see, I can truly receive
The talents and gifts from You

The focus on detail can become so small
That it becomes difficult to see
The growth and the purpose that beckons and calls
To build true unity

I won't let you take me off my game
When I say that, I'm being sincere
For God has given me a new timeframe
The focus is finally clear

The big picture is really what matters you see
For details both large and small
For a positive ripple that begins with me
And continues to consistently install

All things Christ-like, all things pure
That allow me to love and forgive
And truly and realistically help me to endure
And not be held captive

To represent my Savior and King
And serve Him with all that I am
Past failures, regrets; dangers seen and unseen
He'll provide a bush with a ram

I won't let you take me off my game
I'm looking beyond where you are
My life will never be the same
Next level isn't too far

Why Do People Gotta Be So Mean?

Kay Smith

Police brutality – reality
Fear of what is different – commonality
Benefit of the doubt – invisible
Misuse of power – predictable
Perception – mistake
We just can't catch a break

I don't understand why people gotta be so mean
My soul aches and my heart breaks, every time we are seen,
misunderstood and judged just for simply "being"

My mind won't even let me grasp babies being
shot and people of color harassed
Continuously, consistently, with no reprieve;
just in your face, I can't conceive

911 – constant flack
Fifty shades of gray? Nope. Fifty shades of black.
Why do people gotta be so mean?
When will they just let God back on the scene?

The blood He shed on the cross for me
Is the same color red He shed for "we"
He gave His life for humanity

So why do people gotta be so mean?
Really, they don't; it's a choice that's been hidden in between
Years of being politically correct, but covertly obscene

Unjust times, corrupted by man
From the days of old since time began
Surely this was not the Father's plan

Have we come full circle, with no redemption in sight;
Or will we fall on our knees and get spiritually right?
The last days are here, yet we continue to fight

Lord we need you back on the scene
I don't understand why your people gotta be so mean

Thunder Storms

Kay Smith

Loud and rumbling noise, electricity cracks the sky
Inside I feel it, inside I tremble, inside I
don't feel safe; I have no control
I crawl under the covers, close my eyes and bury my head
The thunder ceases, the lightning dissipates, the
earth is clean and calm, but not my life

The storms are symbolic of my life…blow after blow
Inside I feel it, inside I tremble, inside I
don't feel safe; I have no control
I crawl under the covers, close my eyes and bury my head
The storms keep on raging, I need to face them; I need closure

I pray for peace, I pray for strength, I pray to conquer my fear
I grab my pillow, I open the door and sit; I face the storm
I fall asleep in the midst of the storm and inside I feel it,
I feel peace, I feel strength, I am not afraid of the storm

I watch it and realize I have no control,
but I will have closure as I face the storms;
it's symbolic of my life

Peace

Kay Smith

Being at peace doesn't mean nothing's wrong
Peace can appear in the midst of your chaos
It's a mental state of divine revelation
When God's presence envelops you
And takes you to a place of comfort and safety
And allows you to breathe and relax
His peace is perfect and makes everything right

Spiritual Attack

Kay Smith

My purpose must be important; the angels are fighting on my behalf
I never even considered the impact I might have

God chose me long before my conception to be a child of His
Satan saw what God saw and knew I could not live

He tried to take me out in every situation
But the God of glory wrote my story without any hesitation

My mother had no clue that being spiritually weak
Would one day produce a pathway for a child so mild and meek

That child would have a child and plant a spiritual seed
So the young child would soon mature and become anointed to lead

Up above me I imagine blazing swords of glory
Fighting for me and that child so we can enlarge our territory

The struggle is not against flesh and blood, but against authorities
Our weapon is the word of God in this we must believe

We must put on the full armor and take Him at His word
The breastplate of truth and the shield of
faith for gifts that must be stirred

The spiritual attack will not hold back, the goal is to make us cower
But to survive and thrive with a life in Christ,
we must stand firm in His power

Ill Intentions

Kay Smith

The Pharisees had ill intentions, but Jesus didn't entertain them
He saw, felt and experienced it firsthand, but
He was about His Father's business

Evil comes dressed in every outfit you can imagine
I see, feel and experience it firsthand – those ill intentions
And modern-day Pharisees

I fall prey to ill intention, it consumes me at times
I lose focus and drift from my Father's business
It hinders my faith, but

Divine intervention covers and protects me
I see, feel and experience it firsthand
I am delivered from ill intentions…

I am free to be about my Father's business

His Bruises for My Bruises

Kay Smith

Bruised heart beating in the womb before my introduction
Beaten and bruised in the tomb, He was
just following divine instruction
His bruises for my bruises was a sacrifice
planned thousands of years ago
The good news is that His obedience freed me
from becoming extremely mental
Satan tried to kill me, but His stripes healed
me and let my journey begin
On the path to the truth that began in my youth
that those bruises would cleanse all my sins
Being conceived in the way that I was, definitely
paved the way for my demise
But glory to God that He broke through the
façade and opened my spiritual eyes
His bruises for my bruises, I'm so grateful to
Him, my Savior died to break every curse
The lifter of my head, the blood that He shed
allowed me to shift and reverse
Bruised heart mending, salvation unending,
everything I am is from you
Thank you for strength, thank you for grace
and mercies each day that are new

Humility

Kay Smith

Not being invited to the table is humbling
Whether you deserve a seat or not
But be at peace knowing your Father sees
For with humility comes wisdom
And with pride comes disgrace
Repent and be free to receive forgiveness
From entitlement and being void of light
For the table you seek - is His
So humbly bow and wait

Default

Kay Smith

As I become more seasoned in my life with Christ
There are times I find myself at a place of default
Returning to old habits, ways, thoughts and behaviors
Yet, He is worthy and worth our sacrifice and obedience
Don't default to a lesser standard
No, evolve and escape to freedom

Reflection

Kay Smith

Night falls…
I close my eyes and brush my teeth, the day is done
I don't want to see the damage in my reflection
Mean thoughts, bad choices and lapses in judgment
Are waiting in my reflection
I force myself to look into myself
I stare in disbelief; I am empty

Morning comes…
I close my eyes and brush my teeth, a new day begins
I own up to the mean thoughts, bad choices and lapses in judgment
I ask for forgiveness and for the strength to forgive myself
I open my eyes, my spiritual eyes
I stare with confidence; I am made in His image

I trust Him to help me see through the reflection to my purpose

Imperfect Me

Kay Smith

Imperfect, inadequate, incomplete
I, I, I... I can't compete
It's not about I; it's all about You
Perfect and pure, I must give you your due
Quietly nudging me, but never judging me
Patiently waiting, but never begrudgingly
You're a gentleman, its been a labor of love
Seventy times seven my sins erased with your blood
Imperfect me can't be anything without perfect you
Many times I've tried, but I couldn't subdue
All the anger, the doubt, the bitterness and fear
Even though I knew you were always so near
As I strayed away from your bosom,
Your divine protection and favor
Your unconditional love for me never once wavered
You sent people to help me and encourage me through
All the things that went wrong and when I gave up on you
You stayed steadfast and sure that I'd come out intact
And hit my stride never once looking back
For the imperfection I see comes from the pit of hell
But the perfection that is You is where I must dwell
I must place everything at the foot of your throne
I, I, I... I can't do it alone
It's not about I; it's all about You
For you have designed my divine breakthrough
Imperfect, inadequate and incomplete
The devil is a liar, I smell defeat

Full Circle

Kay Smith

Circles are cycles
I have been...
the accused and the accuser
the neglected and the neglectful
the guiltless and the guilty
the brokenhearted and the heartbreaker
unashamed and shamed
the motherless and the mothering
I have come full circle
The cycles must cease

Family

Kay Smith

We are blood, but not connected
Memories are there, but so infected
Relationships scarred, so disrespected
Sharing a space, but so neglected

Family is what we make it
Prayerful beginning, don't forsake it
Winging it, you can't just fake it
Total dysfunction, I just can't take it

After years of being on my own
How to love, never shown
Seeds of wisdom never sown
Functional relationships, never known

Holidays come and holidays go
Being alone is all I know
Given a life so invisible
"I don't deserve", is my motto

Sincere concern and love so true
This was never once my view
Unhappiness and silence is what came through
But days of old I can't renew

You are the one that keeps me sane
From brokenness, I can't explain
Your angels keep me, despite my pain,
My disregard and my disdain

Your love so complete and oh so pure
Lets me know I can endure
Despite my family being obscure
Jesus loves me of this I'm sure

We are blood, new generation
God knew this at my creation
Brand new heart, operation
Second chance - celebration

Finding My Place

Kay Smith

I am unique; fearfully and wonderfully made
But I wasn't taught that or told that
I wasn't raised in that way
I was taught to drive a car and work a job
And that education was important
But when it came to spiritual things
My life was so distorted

Orphaned at conception
An impulsive act that soon would come to regret
No thought given to consequence, no plan for direction
but God knew what was to come next

At such a young age the foundation was laid
God consistently poured into me
And even through all the abuse and neglect
He knew where my place would be

But how much farther would I be
If I had been shown the truth
That God loved me so that He died for me
His creation is the proof

All these years of finding my place
In a place that is not my home
Has been such a test, but I did my best
Raising up me on my own

But I wasn't alone and I came to realize
That in finding me I needed to find You
It took years of searching to open my eyes
And begin to believe in your truth

You were always there, I just needed to trust
That what you said in your word was for me
You see, I didn't feel loved which seemed so unjust
Because I didn't choose to be

As I continue to learn to find where I fit
And be grateful for the gifts I've been given
My life to Christ I will submit
And continue to be purpose driven

Reminding Redeemer

Kay Smith

Redeemed by you with the price of your life
Yet I still struggle with why...
...I am undeserving

No matter how many times I turn my back on you
or how far I stray
I am reminded of redemption

Daily you flood me with your love, mercy, grace and favor
Reminding me that you are here for me
And that I am your daughter

I am redeemed
And I am ready
to step into my purpose

Current Mood

Kay Smith

There are troubled spaces in every part of my life
At home, at work and at church
I feel some kind of way

Frustration is frequently visited by tears
The tears turn into anger and second guessing
It makes me feel some kind of way

Thoughts are overwhelming; I continue to sift through them
I can't quite pin point their origin, but
I feel some kind of way

But my thoughts are not facts; deal with the facts
The fact, is that I re-visit injustice
And it makes me feel some kind of way

Injustice can be debilitating and injures so many
But His word is the answer for undeserved hurt
I feel some kind of way

One so innocent and pure, shed His blood for me
I am anything but those things
And it makes me feel some kind of way

Current mood – I am undeserving, but I am beyond grateful
His sacrifice makes me feel divinely loved and cared for
And for that...

I feel some kind of way

Celebration

Kay Smith

I'm not where I desire to be,
but that place continues to change
And I always fall short
Yet, He pushes me to celebrate persevering

Digging through layers piled on by others has been exhausting
Retreat and withdrawal have been my companions
I'm tired of being the only one there for me
But He knows how I feel and quietly motivates me to celebrate me

Progress to the mindset of Christ has been glacial
The dance of life has gotten in the way
But He won't let me quit
He pushes me to celebrate the growth

I've come to the realization that Satan wants
me to minimize my growth
But maturing in Christ is cause for celebration
He is pleased with my change, my progress
and my growth to get through me - to me

I will celebrate new life in Christ
My journey continues…

Lightning Source UK Ltd.
Milton Keynes UK
UKHW041833271222
414494UK00012B/167/J